M000202827

DEEPER THAN WORK

How Women of Color Can Make
More Money, Have More Impact,
and Thrive in the Corporate World

Dorianne St Fleur

Deeper Than Work
How Women of Color Can Make More Money, Have More Impact,
and Thrive in the Corporate World

ISBNs:
978-1-7373155-0-6 (print)
978-1-7373155-1-3 (eBook)

Library of Congress Control Number: 2021910821

Because of the dynamic nature of the internet, any web addresses or links contained in this book may have changed since publication and may no longer be valid.

The views expressed in this work are solely those of the author.

Quantity sales are available upon request by corporations, associations, academic institutions, and other organizations. For more information, contact the author at hello@doriannestfleur.co.

For additional resources to help you implement the strategies shared in this book, visit www.deeperthanwork.com/resources

Printed in the United States of America

This book is dedicated to the glass breakers, dragon slayers, and game changers of the past, present, and future. You matter. You belong. You win.

Contents

Acknowledgements

This book would not be possible without my village.

To my husband, Marc, thank you for being my number one fan and giving me the freedom to be who I'm called to be.

To the best dancer I know and the sassiest, classiest daughter in the world, Victoria, thank you for motivating me. Everything I do is for you.

To my mom, Patsy, thank you for pushing me to always operate from a place of excellence.

To my dad, Philip, thank you for the constant reminders to make myself proud.

To Taisha, thank you for putting up with my many meltdowns. You've been helping me get out of my own way since our freshman year at Spelman and I don't take that for granted.

To Isi, thank you for all of the prayers and the pep talks. I'm so grateful we found each other.

To Shaleia and Jamila, thank you for the love, the laughs, and your friendship. I'm grateful to know you both.

To Bola, you're the first person, besides my husband, who demanded I write this book. I'll be forever grateful. Thank you.

To my coaches and mentors, thank you for pouring into me.

To the YCG team, Kayme, Kristie, Khadija, and Shauntelle, I wouldn't be here without you. Thank you.

To every single client, student, and collaborator who has been part of the Career Girl Nation since 2015, thank you from the bottom of my heart. Special shout out to my OG clients, Alicia, DaKenya, and Erica. You've been riding with me since the very beginning, and I'll never forget that.

To Sophia B. Packard and Harriet E. Giles, thank you for Spelman College.

To the late Dean Zenobia L. Hikes, thank you for introducing me to my purpose.

To every Spelman woman from April 11, 1881 to the present, you are my inspiration.

To me, you go girl. Keep killing it.

Most importantly, thank you, Jesus.

Introduction

Deeper Than Work: How Women of Color Can Make More Money, Have More Impact, and Thrive in the Corporate World was created to be culturally relevant to Black, Indigenous, Hispanic/Latina, Asian, and Pacific Islander women.

As you read it, I hope you'll understand how essential a fulfilling career is to a fulfilling life. What you do for a living is way more than just work. Your career impacts your mental, physical, spiritual, and financial well-being. If you're unhappy at work, you'll likely be unhappy in life.

This book is intentionally *not* inundated with statistics, charts, and research about women of color in the corporate world. While data is useful in certain contexts, for what we're trying to achieve here - equipping women of color with the strategies needed to thrive in the corporate world - it really doesn't add to the conversation.

Not to mention, I've already gone through the data at length and can boil all the facts and figures down to this: For various reasons ranging from lack of culturally relevant development and programming to systemic racism, there are pay and leadership gaps for women of color in the corporate world. We are not paid, promoted, and amplified in a way that's aligned with our talent, credentials, and contributions.

Instead, the perspectives, stories, and strategies I share are based on my interactions with mid to senior-level women of color across thousands of hours of coaching clients, facilitating online community groups, and working in human resources.

Since you're reading this book, you've likely experienced how the corporate world can be a cold, hard place for women of color. Maybe you're questioning whether it's even possible to have a fulfilling career where you have the kind of impact, influence, and income that you desire.

If you're anything like me, you may have been taught the only way to climb to the highest heights of success in the corporate world is to strip away all the distinctive, interesting, and colorful parts of yourself. You may also feel as a woman of color, that there's a cap on how much success you can have and no matter how hard you work or how much you contribute, it will never be enough for you to get the recognition and respect you deserve. I want you to know it's possible for you to show up fully and completely while contributing highly impactful work.

Leveraging my expertise as a human resources executive and workplace inclusion consultant, I've taught high-achieving women how to reinvent themselves and their careers, so they can master the corporate world and live their best lives.

I spent over 15 years at companies like Goldman Sachs, AT&T, and Google and learned how to successfully navigate the corporate world. I cultivated a career that allows me to consistently develop and sharpen my skills, build long-lasting and mutually beneficial relationships, thrive in environments that allow me to make a massive impact, receive the recognition and acknowledgment that I deserve, and make the kind of money aligned with my contributions. However, my career hasn't always been this way.

In 2010, I experienced the most harrowing and toxic season of my entire career. I spent 12 months in an environment where I felt like I was being rejected and like I didn't belong. It eventually led to a steep decline in my ability to perform. The more I was sidelined, the more I would make mistakes. The more mistakes I made caused my boss to feel justified in her treatment of me.

I lost all semblance of who I was. I didn't have anyone I could turn to for support or guidance. I felt ostracized and cast to the side at every turn, especially by the other Black woman on the team who I thought would've been an ally.

I was on a merry-go-round of failure, and it wouldn't stop spinning long enough to allow me to exit gracefully. It all culminated with me being laid off.

It felt like all of the successes I had ever experienced in my career were just distant memories, and I had no clue how I was going to change things. I spent the next 13 months unemployed. When I wasn't sitting on my living room couch binge-watching random TV shows on Netflix and eating my feelings, I was interviewing all over Manhattan, New York trying to morph into whichever version of myself I thought the recruiters and hiring managers wanted to see. I'd lost sight of who I was and what I wanted. My career was unrecognizable. Then, by God's grace, something clicked.

In order to push through this season of my life, I would have to move from a space of rejection to a space of reinvention. I wasn't just going to launch a job search process. I was going to revive my entire career.

That's exactly what I did. In less than 30 days, I'd picked myself up, dusted myself off, and landed a higher-paying, more senior position at a great company. I did it my way and on my terms. Landing a dream job was just the first step in the journey of reviving my career. I committed to unapologetically showing up as myself no matter what. I went from feeling rejected, unsupported, undervalued, and unfulfilled to falling in love with the work I do.

All of this led me to where I am now. I get to help other women of color experience these same shifts.

I've had the opportunity to work with mid to senior-level women at companies all over the United States, Canada, the Caribbean, and England. My thoughts on women of color at work and inclusive workplaces have been featured in major publications and TV shows such as "Black Enterprise," "Fast Company," and "The Doctors." None of this would've been possible if I was still stuck hiding my value and shrinking away from who I was and what I genuinely wanted.

My purpose is to share the lessons I've learned so you can apply them to your career. The truth is you can cultivate a career in which you bring the very best of yourself and still have all the impact, influence, and, of course, income that you deserve.

This book will show you how.

With love,
Dorianne

PART 1

The Thriver Mentality

CHAPTER 1

Get Your Mind Right

The single most powerful prerequisite to success is the ability to change the way you think.

ONE PIECE OF advice I give to women of color questioning the current state of their career is this: The road to designing the kind of career where you can thrive is a mind game more than anything else. Yes, you can learn all the career development strategies and master the latest success tools and tips, but to make more money, increase your impact, and avoid losing your sanity or your identity while doing it, you have to master your mind.

This is the one thing I wish I would have understood the moment I entered the corporate world. In the summer of 2005, I left Spelman College, an all-women's historically Black institution, and set out to blaze new trails in corporate America. I was 21 and starting my career as an operations analyst at an international investment bank in Manhattan, New York. I was in an industry, and at a company, that was not all-women and definitely not all-Black. I went from an environment that was safe, validating, and celebratory of my very existence as a Black woman, to one that felt precarious, uninviting, and at times, like my Black womanhood was a scarlet letter I was carrying.

Until that point, my life experiences had been predominantly Black. My parents migrated from Jamaica right before I was born and I grew up in a middle-class Caribbean neighborhood in Brooklyn, New York. I attended Black schools, a Black church, and had Black friends. My upbringing taught me how to love and appreciate who I was. I was proud of being from Brooklyn, my Jamaican heritage, being Black, and being a woman. With all this pride, I didn't notice a blind spot had formed. Since I was always one of many, I had no clue how to navigate being *the only one*. I had never been treated as "other." That is, until I entered corporate America.

At first, it was very subtle and, I'd like to believe, unintentional. When people would be idolized and cheered as they proudly named their Ivy League alma mater, I would feel a slight twinge of embarrassment as their brows furrowed when I mentioned my college - which they'd never heard of. I would dread sharing my vacation plans as the interest left my co-worker's faces listening to me talk about my holiday weekend spent in Prospect Park in comparison to their stories of spending summers in the Hamptons or the South of France. With each slight, no matter how subtle, I felt my experiences mattered less than theirs. Like I was the exception instead of the norm. I became insecure about my background and my socioeconomic status.

Additionally, when I looked at all the people who were climbing the ladder and getting access to senior leadership, there was hardly anyone who looked like me. In a department of tens of thousands of employees, I was able to count the number of Black women leaders on one hand. The vice-presidents, managing directors, and board members were overwhelmingly white men. The people who were influencing and making decisions were white men. Most of the women who managed to break into senior leadership were white. It made me question the likelihood of me being able to make the corporate climb.

Before then, I never saw my upbringing, gender, or race as factors that could keep me from succeeding. However, within months of starting my new job, my mentality was beginning to shift. I spent the next few years overcompensating for the areas in which I thought I was lacking. I attempted to work, dress, speak, and act the way everyone else did. My goal was to assimilate into the culture by any means necessary. It worked. I was promoted quickly and excelled.

On the surface, it seemed like my career hit a comfortable stride. But deep down, the doubts I had about how I fit in the professional world I worked so hard to conform to were chipping away at my pride and confidence.

Despite my waning self-esteem, I was able to complete my first major career transition. In 2010, I moved from client operations into my dream role as an HR Generalist. I was on cloud nine when I got the offer to join the new team. For the first time in my career, I felt like I had the opportunity to do work that genuinely aligned with my strengths and interests. I was fielding phone calls from employees about their careers, ghostwriting team memos on behalf of leaders, and strategizing on the development needs for high performing employees. The first few weeks on the job were off to a great start.

Fast forward three months and everything changed. What started off as my dream job quickly turned into a nightmare. Although I still enjoyed the work I was doing, it became clear that I wasn't on the right team. It was full of cliques, overly competitive, and had zero tolerance for human error. Based on the intensity of the team, you'd think we were heart surgeons saving lives, instead of human resources professionals.

To make matters worse, the team was led by the worst manager I've ever experienced. This woman had no business managing people. She was moody, gave special treatment to her favorites, and lacked the emotional intelligence necessary to effectively develop her team. She had the ability to instantly induce anxiety without saying a word. As soon as I saw her face, I would tense anticipating her critical gaze, condescending tone, and dismissive mannerisms.

I regularly worked 50-60 hours per week and wasn't allowed to leave for the day until after my boss did. If I had a question or felt stuck on something I was working on, I would try my best to avoid asking clarifying questions since my boss would become visibly irritated if she had to repeat herself.

The relationship with my colleagues didn't help. We were a team of 13 and were fairly diverse across race, gender, sexual orientation, and parental status. It could have been a dynamic experience, but it wasn't because my colleagues were also trying their best to navigate the traumatic environment. The team culture was full of fear and distrust.

I also had to deal with the fiery darts of the only other Black woman on the team. When I first met her, I thought we were going to be fast friends. We had similar taste in clothes, both married, and both Beyoncé stans. Before I joined the team, I had an informational interview with her to learn more about the role. I believe she was instrumental in getting me hired which is why I was shocked at how she treated me once I joined the team. She spoke to me in disrespectful ways, talked about me behind my back with my colleagues, and questioned my intelligence at every turn.

I was anxious every moment that I was at work. When I wasn't working, I would be uneasy thinking about the next time I'd be there. I couldn't concentrate on my tasks and regularly made mistakes. The more mistakes I made caused my boss to feel justified in the way she was treating me. I felt like no matter how hard I tried, I couldn't catch a break. There was an instance when one of the formulas on a spreadsheet I was working on was incorrect. Even though I'd double, and triple checked the spreadsheet before handing it off to my manager, there was an error I hadn't noticed. Instead of walking me through the mistake and teaching me how to ensure I didn't repeat it next time, she publicly berated me. I spent the afternoon hiding in the bathroom drowning in a pool of my tears.

My inner insecurities began to spill out onto the surface. I wondered if I'd gone to a better school, made more money, or looked differently if my manager would respond to me another way. I changed the way I talked to mirror the phrasing, cadence, and vocal fry I heard from the influencers on the team. I changed the way I dressed and the jewelry I wore. I tried to act like them. None of it worked. I was still cast to the side. I internalized the rejection as character flaws. I thought, *I'm not accepted when I'm myself. I'm not accepted when I'm like you, so there is obviously something wrong with me.*

I constantly had negative thoughts about my job. I visualized getting fired. I had dreams about being reprimanded. I battled anxiety, depression, weight gain, and strained relationships with my loved ones because of my inability to process the emotions I experienced on the job. The few positive thoughts about myself I had left were obliterated. I forgot I was smart and had gotten accepted into every college I applied to. I forgot I was an amazing communicator and that I learned quickly. I forgot I was a top performer and people liked my sense of humor and personality. All the things that I knew to be true about myself were stripped away. I had no recollection of my value and my worth.

After 12 months of agony, all the mistakes, awkward email exchanges with my manager, and overall team misalignment finally caught up with me. I was laid off. The official line was that they were restructuring the team and my role was now redundant. In retrospect, it was the best thing that could have happened at that time. God provided a way of escape from a space that was literally and figuratively killing me. Yet the same thoughts still remained: *I'm not smart enough. I don't have the right experience. I can't make it in a high-performance environment. I don't belong in the corporate world.*

When I think back on that season of my career, I want to shake some sense into myself. I wish I could see I wasn't the problem. I was still the high achiever I'd always been. My ability or skills hadn't changed. It was my mindset. If I could go back in time to the moment after I was laid off, here's what I would say to myself: *This sucks. You've had to deal with this horrible environment for so long and you didn't even have the opportunity to leave on your terms. Now, you have two options. You can get caught up in who's to blame for the current state of your career, or you can decide to own your actions from this moment forward. You can either settle into your trauma or you can walk into your triumph.*

Since I can't go back in time and give myself this sage advice, I'll give it to you instead. Women of color experience racism, bullying, sexism, ageism, xenophobia and so much more at work. Being trapped in a cycle of mental torment, self-doubt, crippling anxiety, and dissatisfaction doesn't have to be your reality. That part can shift as soon as your beliefs do.

We all have occasional negative thoughts floating around in our brains. These thoughts are influenced by who we're around, what we watch, and what information we consume. *That person is smarter than me. She's better looking. I'm a terrible public speaker. I have imposter syndrome. I'll never earn more money than I do now.* We sometimes elevate these thoughts to truth status by replaying them over and over again until we adopt them as facts.

If I didn't believe I was inferior in that toxic environment, there most likely would have been a different outcome. Instead of internalizing failure and rejection, I could have taken online classes to fill skill gaps. I could have sought out a mentor to help guide me. I could have stood up for myself when I was being disrespected. I could have thought *I'm not inferior, so let me get to the root of what the issue is and turn this reality around. If I can't, then I will leave. I'm good enough to thrive somewhere else.*

I wish I could say I learned how important shifting my beliefs were once I was laid off, but that's not what happened. Instead, I was unemployed for 13 months and spent most of that time nursing wounds of unworthiness. I couldn't see past my team's rejection. Even though I had five years of evidence showing I was great at what I did, and I knew what I was doing, I chose to ignore it all and focus on the negative circumstances of the previous year.

I would describe the first 12 months of my job search as aimless. I had no confidence in my ability to land the roles I applied for. If I got an interview, I was so nervous about how to explain being laid off that my mind would go blank. I literally couldn't remember what I'd accomplished, how to do the job, or why I was suited for the role. There were even a few months where I decided I was done with the corporate world altogether and concluded that it was time for me to reinvent myself as a mixologist. I was genuinely committed to this career path. I enrolled in the New York Bartending School and after 35 hours in a hands-on learning experience about the art of mixology, I became a certified bartender. I was all set to embark on my new career until I realized that bartenders were expected to be outgoing, tactful, and have impeccable stamina. Armed with this knowledge, I decided it was probably in my best interest to go back to a position more suitable to my personality in corporate America.

In my 13th month of unemployment, something finally clicked. I realized that if I was ever going to make any headway in my job search, I would have to be intentional with my process. I'd need to be consistent with my research, get organized with my applications, and strategically prepare for my interviews. In order to do that though, I had to address the thoughts and feelings about myself and my career head on. I spent time in prayer, meditated on scriptures related to faith, and started journaling. I decided I was done feeling sorry for myself. I was going to reprogram my beliefs and reintroduce myself to the high achiever that I'd always been. This decision was the turning point in my job search. I thought differently. I talked differently. I behaved differently. This completely changed the tone I took on my resume and the dynamic in my interviews. I allowed myself to shine. Within 30 days, I went from 12 months of no job prospects to considering multiple job offers. I landed my dream job with a more senior title and higher salary.

Every negative thought about who I was, what I deserved, and what I could do disappeared when I shifted the story I told myself. Instead of thinking, *I'm not a top performer, and that's why I was laid off,* I thought, *I have a track record of achievement. I've been promoted and pulled off a huge career transition.* Instead of thinking, *I'm not good enough and my experiences aren't valuable,* I thought, *I have been given specific gifts and talents that are lined up with my calling. All I have is all I need.*

My new beliefs helped me make better decisions. I started thinking, *I'm going to apply for that job. I'm going to have this conversation. I'm going to go to this networking event. I'm going to put myself out there.* My actions were different which created a new reality. I didn't change. I was still the same person. What changed were my beliefs. I finally got my mind right.

If you're not happy with where you currently are in your career, I want to suggest that you take some time to not only focus on changing the external circumstances, but also work on getting down to the core of what beliefs are keeping you from stepping into your new season. This will help you do the mental work necessary to change your reality.

Career Reflection

How have thoughts about yourself and your career shaped your current reality?

What beliefs have you adopted as fact as a result of a negative experience in your career?

How have these beliefs kept you from stepping to the next level in your career?

Pick one unwanted circumstance you're currently experiencing in your career. What thoughts, feelings, stories, decisions, and actions can you change to produce a new reality?

CHAPTER 2

Confidence is a Choice

Your ability to discern advice you should keep and advice you should throw away will be the difference between your success and your mediocrity.

'VE SPENT THOUSANDS of hours coaching high achievers through various career milestones. No matter how different their backgrounds and goals may be, there's one thing many have in common. At some point in their careers, they acted on advice received from someone they trust. Listening to those who want to see you win isn't a bad thing, but some advice can cause more harm than good.

What I've found through client conversations and in my own experience, is sometimes what's buried underneath the well-intentioned advice, statistics, and anecdotes we get from our loved ones are their fears, insecurities, and limitations. When we internalize these things, it causes us to operate from a place of lack and mediocrity instead of showing up fully in our greatness.

One of the biggest regrets I have from my time at Spelman was not taking advantage of their study abroad program. Before going to college, my international travel experience consisted of a few visits to see family in Jamaica, Canada, and London. Each trip was brief, and I, like most children, was tethered to my parents. While I'm grateful to have been exposed to international travel in those early years, I had yet to have an independent, immersive global experience.

I was thrilled when I found out I was eligible to apply for a semester abroad in Africa during my junior year. I shared the news with my community, and to my surprise, I was peppered with questions riddled with doubt and anxiety about Malaria, clean drinking water, and kidnappings. One person even made me feel guilty for wanting to "leave them" to pursue the program. Just like that, the flames of my excitement were smothered. Though I was disappointed, I decided they were right, and I chose to stay put. My well-meaning community succeeded in projecting their fears, limitations, and self-interests onto me. I didn't even apply for the program.

A semester abroad would've allowed me to expand my academic worldview, become more open-minded, and be more adaptable. All things that would benefit my career years later. I've been to Africa twice since I graduated college, but I can't help but wonder how experiencing the continent studying abroad could have impacted my career and my life. What if I had thrown away the bad advice, albeit loving, from my confidantes? What if I had chosen to follow my heart instead of other people's fears? So many what ifs.

I wish I could say that was the last time I allowed other people's trauma, experiences, and perceptions to keep me from stepping out of my comfort zone and living with no limits. I've heard similar sentiments from the women I work with. What I've found is that the stories we tell ourselves as a result of the restrictions others place on us are mostly rooted in three categories that I call Collective Limiting Beliefs.

Collective Limiting Belief #1: We Have to Be Better Than Everyone Else

There's a saying that was deeply ingrained in my psyche for most of my career: Black women have to work twice as hard to get half as far. Other women of color I've spoken to have heard some version of this for their cultural background as well. Whether it's an Asian woman recalling how she was told that to be successful at work, she must be perfect or risk being a disgrace. A Latina woman remembering being told to put her head down, be diligent and let her work speak for itself. Or an Indigenous woman recounting the times she was told to be grateful for the opportunities she has and not "rock the boat." It all boils down to the same takeaway: Your factory setting isn't good enough. Be better. Do better.

This advice has been handed down to us from our foremothers to protect us. They were shut out from many rooms since the inception of work. They've had to sit back and watch as they were passed over for promotions and opportunities they were rightfully deserving of. In hopes of preventing us from having the same outcomes, they've given us this advice from a place of love and sincerity.

We've come a long way from generations before us. On average, we're making more money and have climbed to higher rungs on the corporate ladder than our mothers and grandmothers. What's interesting is even with all of our progress, research shows women of color still make up just 9% of senior manager/ director positions, 6% of vice president positions, 5% of senior vice president positions, and 3% of C-suite positions in corporate America (*Women in the Workplace 2020*, 2020). Not to mention, there's now a generation of women who have normalized working themselves into anxiety, depression, burnout, and physical illness.

Based on the data, as well as the experiences of women I work with across various levels and industries, it would seem that the advice we've been given, while well-intentioned, is incomplete. The stories my clients share illustrate that the goal posts for women of color are constantly moving. Even when we're working twice as hard, or trying to be perfect, or putting our heads down and letting our work speak for itself. This advice can only take you so far. What got you here, won't take you to your next level.

One of the first exercises I take my clients through is putting together their professional receipts, a.k.a. their "body of work." It's a carefully curated list of all the accomplishments, accolades, and credentials they've garnered throughout their careers. Seeing their achievements laid out before their eyes in black and white is awe-inspiring. When they realize how much they've done and how qualified they are, they begin to shed the notion they have to keep working themselves into burnout or continue to accept getting half of what they truly deserve. This is the beginning of the shift.

It doesn't take us operating at 200% to make strides in our careers. In fact, even if we operated at 85%, it's likely we'd still be working circles around others. Why? We are educated, qualified, experienced, resilient, and flexible. We are excellent. This excellence doesn't take working twice as hard for us to succeed. What it takes is being intentional and strategic about how and where we show up.

Collective Limiting Belief #2: We Need Approval

Have you ever been told that in order to climb the corporate ladder, you'll need to master the art of getting people to accept and approve of you? If you have, you're not alone. Many of us believe we need to contort ourselves to make it easier for supe-riors, colleagues, and clients to approve of our existence in the corporate world. The idea that someone has to approve your value for you to succeed is a toxic belief that has to go.

There is absolutely no human on this Earth who has the power to approve the space you take up. You are fearfully and wonderfully made, and you were approved from the moment you were born. You were specifically put here to do great work. While it's true that you need support, allyship, mentorship, and sponsorship as you ascend in your career, that's not the same as needing someone to tolerate, accept, and validate your existence.

Let me let you in on a little secret: You belong in every room in which you find yourself. You belong in the corporate world. Your perspective is valuable. Your perspective is needed. Whether or not other people approve of that fact doesn't make it any less true.

When I was in that toxic work environment, I wanted the approval of everyone around me so badly. I wanted validation. I wanted them to tell me I was good enough, that I belonged, and they liked me. Imagine how the dynamic would have shifted if I walked into those spaces saying: "Things aren't progressing the way I want. I need your help and your support." Instead, my self-talk sounded more like, *I've now dressed like you and changed the way I talk and act. Do you like me now?*

When you move from a place of needing validation and approval into a space where you're thinking, *I'm here so I already belong*, you show up differently. If you were hired or promoted into a role, given a team to lead, assigned a big opportunity, or asked to speak on a panel, know you belong there.

Think about a diamond. It is precious. There's a brilliance about it. It shines. Those facts don't change just because the diamond gets tossed out the window and ends up under some rocks and dirt, and some stray animal starts using it as a chew toy. Just because the animal can't or won't appreciate the value of the object in its presence doesn't change the fact that the diamond is *still* valuable. How much more valuable are you than a diamond? It doesn't matter if the people you work with see it or not. Accept and approve yourself. When you do, you can enter into tough spaces and say, "Okay, this is what I need from you to succeed. This is the kind of allyship and support I'm expecting."

Collective Limiting Belief #3: We Have Imposter Syndrome

Spoiler alert: You are not an imposter.

I don't care what anyone says. I never will agree that when we feel incapable or hesitant, we're suffering from imposter syndrome. I'm not saying it's not real. I'm not saying it doesn't exist. What I am saying is just because you feel uncertain and you're getting feedback on areas you need to develop; it doesn't mean you are an imposter or a failure. As I've mentioned in the previous chapter, what you believe about yourself has a huge impact on how you show up. Believing you're a fraud does not help you thrive at work.

You are fully capable of breaking through the ceilings placed over your head. Unfortunately, it won't be without having to deal with unfairness, inequity, exclusion, racism, and oppression. Is there any surprise that you feel anxious and uncertain? The labels you give yourself can make or break your career. When you oversimplify your experience as a woman of color in the workplace and chalk it up to imposter syndrome, you're ignoring what's actually happening.

When I was battling the toxic work environment, I believed on a deep level that I was the source of my issues. I didn't think about my environment. I didn't think about my lack of support. It was all my fault. I was an imposter. I was a fraud.

I'd love to host a roundtable with the people from that toxic team and my colleagues who worked with me on the first role I had after I was unemployed. I bet their recollections of me would be as different as night and day. One group would say I was quiet, hesitant, and couldn't navigate a Microsoft Excel spreadsheet to save my life. While the other group would say I was confident, poised, and an Excel whiz. The time between each of these groups working with me was only 13 months, and I spent most of that time feeling sorry for myself and not gaining new skills. So, what changed? The way I saw myself.

I believe that confidence is a choice. I've seen it play out in my life and in the lives of my clients. When I landed my new role after being laid off, I made the conscious decision to remind myself often that I belonged. I showed up to work every day like I owned the place. If there was any issue or any disconnect, I'd ask myself, *What support do I need? What about the environment needs to change? What skills do I need to build?* I played to my strengths and put this whole business of inferiority and being an imposter behind me.

It's not a bad thing to get advice as you navigate your career. It's important to seek wise counsel. What's important is to remember, all advice isn't created equal. Sometimes the advice we receive can cause us to adopt one (or more) of these limiting beliefs. You must become a master at deciding what you'll keep and what you'll throw away.

You and your career are limitless. The key to tapping into your potential is to reject anything (or anyone) who tries to make you believe otherwise.

Career Reflection

Who do you seek for career advice? How have they helped you either remove self-imposed limits or remain stagnant?

What can you do to determine which advice you should keep and which advice you should throw away?

Which of the three collective limiting beliefs have you previously ascribed? How will your views change moving forward?

How would your career look if you removed the limits you've placed on yourself?

CHAPTER 3

The Path You're Called to Follow

The most tragic thing you can do is waste the little time you have here on Earth trying to live someone else's life.

ONE OF THE most important career (and life) lessons I've learned is you can't measure your success by someone else's yardstick. It sounds simple, but it's so simple it's easy to miss. Have you thought about how you define success? Have you outlined what it looks like for you and what will happen when you finally arrive at that point?

Most of the women I work with initially answer these questions with a resounding "NO." Instead, they find themselves going after success markers they're not even sure they want. They've blindly pursued degrees, job titles, and accolades without first taking time to uncover what they truly want.

I was working with a client a few years ago, a practicing attorney, who was unfulfilled in her career. As we unpacked the source of her dissatisfaction, she came to a big realization. When she initially decided to pursue her law degree, she did it because someone else said she should.

My parents, family, and friends all told me law was the way to go. I picked the law school a friend of mine suggested. I selected the type of law I'd practice based on the opinion of my professor. For the past 15 years, I've been making decisions in my career not based on what I want but based on what other people told me I should do. Now, I'm here, and I don't feel successful. I don't feel accomplished. People look at me on paper and say, "You're doing amazing things," but when I'm alone with my thoughts and looking in the mirror, I feel far from amazing.

This isn't an isolated case of someone living by everyone else's success markers. I've heard many variations of this same story.

I want to invite you even before you read any further to take a moment to think about what success means for you. What success markers would you like to check off in the next two years, five years, fifteen? How will you know when you've arrived? Without a thorough understanding of your answers to these questions, you'll likely end up going through the motions doing things you think you *should* be doing, and never feeling like you're actually moving the needle forward in your career.

Just because other people are getting master's degrees, are on the accelerated track for promotion, or are working at certain types of companies, it doesn't automatically mean that's the path you're called to follow.

We often get caught up in what I like to call "shoulding on ourselves." It goes a little something like this: *I should have been promoted already. I should have another degree or certification. I should have been at this level in my career by now. I should have had this opportunity. I should be making this amount of money. I should be connected with these people.*

Going down this rabbit hole of all the "shoulds" in your career can leave you feeling trapped and overwhelmed, especially if none of it is what you truly want. Pursuing success markers that aren't yours puts undue stress and pressure on you. If you're not able to meet the artificial demands you've placed on yourself, you feel like a failure.

It's hard to stay motivated if you're trying to keep up with a career path that doesn't belong to you in the first place. It's like you can feel something tugging at you internally, and it causes you to resist. You procrastinate. You second-guess your decisions, and you self-sabotage. More often than not, it's because deep down you know *this is not what I want.*

Success not only looks different for everyone, but it can also look different for the same person depending on the season of their career. How I define a successful career is likely completely different from your definition. Similarly, how I defined success 10 years ago, even five years ago, is completely different from how I define it today. What matters is to root your definition in your truth and not in a pile of shoulds.

There was a time when everyone around me was going to graduate school. They were getting MBAs and other master's degrees, and I thought, *Wait a second. Am I missing something? Why is everyone going to grad school? They're getting accepted into these programs. I should go to grad school too.* I never took the time to consider if this was what I wanted or how it aligned with my overall career goals. Instead, I took my Graduate Record Exam (GRE), researched graduate schools, and enrolled in a program.

I hated it. It was hard for me to juggle a full-time job with part-time school. I couldn't stay motivated to go to classes and didn't connect with the coursework. I spent months stressing myself out trying to make it work and I ultimately dropped out.

I think back on the time I wasted. It was time I'll never get back. I think about the loans I spent years paying back for this unfinished degree. I think about the emotional energy I spent calling myself a quitter and a failure. I had no business being there. That graduate program wasn't even on my path. I didn't need it in the version of success that was aligned with my gifts, talents, and calling.

In addition to keeping money in your pocket and not wasting time, stepping out of the "should trap" and getting clear on what success looks like for you allows you to make quicker, more strategic decisions. When you're clear on what you want, why you want it, and what you need to get it, it's easier to discern the difference between a decision that's aligned with your journey and one that's just a distraction.

Thankfully, I've come a long way since my failed attempt at graduate school. I'm laser-focused on being clear about what success looks like for me in each season of my career and helping the women I work with do the same. If you feel like you lack clarity, or you keep going back and forth about what you need to do next, it's likely you're unclear of what success looks like for you. The key to seamlessly making huge transitions like changing industries, switching companies, or relocating to your dream city is taking the time to consistently check in with your success markers. Ask yourself simple questions like, *What's the larger picture I'm working toward? What's my overall goal? How will I know that this is a good decision?* The answers to these questions can take you far.

Career Reflection

How do you define career success?

What have you pursued or are currently pursuing in your career that's based on what other people said you should be doing?

What are 3 - 5 success markers you'd like to accomplish in the next 12 months of your career?

How will you know when you ultimately have arrived at your destination?

PART 2
The Thriver Shift

CHAPTER 4

Plan to Fill the Gaps

The biggest tragedy in the career of a high achiever is the day they stop learning.

I N MY WORK, I often encounter women who absolutely hate their jobs. To say they are simply surviving their careers doesn't fully describe the space they're in. The reasons range from feeling undervalued, underpaid, or like the work they do is misaligned with their purpose. The good news is that these women have been able to overcome the barriers and obstacles in their way to design the kind of career where they can make more money, have more impact, and thrive. They did it by focusing

41

less on what was wrong with the corporate world and more on focusing on designing their dream career.

The first thing my clients realize when we start working together is that what they've been taught about what it means to have a dream career has either been wrong or incomplete. Having a dream career doesn't have to be like finding a soulmate. The stars don't need to align to create a once-in-a-lifetime opportunity for you to do the work you love. It's possible to have multiple dream jobs throughout your career. It may even be possible to transform your current role into the job of your dreams.

I've created the D.R.E.A.M.™ Job Profile to walk you through the process of designing your dream career so you can go from surviving to thriving.

- D is for Development
- R is for Relationships
- E is for Environment
- A is for Acknowledgement
- M is for Money

In the next few chapters, I'll break down each part of the profile in detail.

Let's start with "D" - **Development.**

One of the challenges I've heard from my clients is that their companies fail to give them access to the kind of coaching and training they need to excel in their roles. Continuous professional development is crucial on the road to climbing the corporate ladder. Rather than stalling your growth as you wait for your company to do right by you, consider taking matters into your own hands by building your development plan.

A customized development plan allows you to intentionally map out your journey as you move toward your career goals. It allows you to think about the kind of impact you want to make and outline what you'll need to do to ensure your resume, skill set, and experiences align with your goals. Your development plan can help you make more strategic decisions and will prevent you from wasting time and money on "growth" opportunities that aren't necessary for your career trajectory. It also helps you to course-correct if you get off track.

After my layoff, I took time to assess the specific skills I wanted to develop to increase my impact in my new job and avoid the same former traps. I combed through feedback I previously received, and I thought about what would make me notable. One skill I focused on was data analysis. Specifically, my ability to use Microsoft Excel. This was the bane of my existence on my old team. I still can remember a particularly condescending conversation between my manager and me in which she questioned my intelligence because I was having trouble with the VLOOKUP function and pivot tables. Being able to master it would serve as personal vindication. I cobbled together an Excel training plan that included enrolling in free courses online, joining user forums, and committing to mastering a suite of common formulas. All my hard work paid off and I was able to turn myself into a data queen. I became known for my Excel skills in my new role, and it was a critical differentiating factor between me and my colleagues.

I've witnessed far too many instances where high achievers treat their career growth and development as an afterthought. Taking time for professional growth can feel like a luxury. Especially if you're facing more pressing issues at work like looming deadlines, chaotic teams, and racism. But when designing a dream career where you consistently increase your income, impact, and influence, professional development must become a priority.

To do this, begin with the end in mind. Ask yourself, *To get to where I want to be in my career, what expertise do I need to develop? What skills do the top performers in my department and/ or company have that I'll need to grow? What experiences will I need to have in order to make a larger impact on my team or in my industry?* Once you're clear on where you want to be, you can create a strategic plan to fill the gaps.

A few years ago, I coached a client through a rough patch in her career. She was the Senior Director of Business Strategy at a non-profit organization based in Washington, D.C. She had all the credentials she needed for the role complete with an Ivy League education. What she didn't have was the foundational managerial skills she needed to lead her team effectively, i.e., delegation, prioritization, and the capacity to build credibility. Her lack of these skills resulted in an insubordinate team that didn't trust her and a supervisor who had lost faith in her ability to perform. To add insult to injury, she also was the target of racially insensitive comments. Her confidence was shot.

The first thing we did was define her objective, which was to become an effective leader and build trust with the team. We then created a development plan focused on building her communication, delegation, and leadership skills. The plan included targeted training on the foundations of leadership, customized coaching designed to prepare her for challenging situations that came up on her team, and strategic mentorship from individuals she identified as top-notch leaders. Within six months, the dynamic on her team was unrecognizable. They'd gone from a group of individual contributors who didn't respect her and often went above her head, to a team of collaborators who understood her role as their leader. She was able to build credibility, trust, and respect. When friction did arise, she had the tools she needed to navigate them without relinquishing her authority. She was successful because she took a strategic approach to develop her skills.

Here's how you can create a strategic development plan of your own.

1. **Assess your goals.** Begin with the end in mind. Think about the goals you've set for the next 6 - 12 months in your career and make a list of the skills required for you to excel at the next level.

2. **Identify your gaps.** Take the time to understand where there are skills gaps between where you are now and where you want to be. Consider speaking with your

manager and looking at job descriptions, so you can compare the skills required with your current abilities. Understanding where there may be gaps will help you identify the type of skill-building you'll need.

3. **Prioritize your growth.** Focusing on a development plan with too many moving parts can do more harm than good. As a rule of thumb, try focusing on up to three development skills at a time. Divide the skills you've listed into two categories: 1) skills that will allow you to provide immediate impact, and 2) skills that will be useful for you to build a bit further down the road.

4. **Create your learning plan.** Once you have assessed, identified, and prioritized your development needs, you're ready to solidify your learning plan. Map out *how* you will improve your skills. Options include completing online courses, enrolling in a formal training program or certification program, and hiring a coach.

Career Reflection

How can creating a strategic development plan help you increase your impact at work?

How does your current skill set align with the priorities of your team, company, and/or department?

How can the skills you've gained from past work experiences help you with preparing for your next level?

What skills or knowledge gaps do you need to bridge to be ready for the next phase of your career?

CHAPTER 5

Maximize Your Impact

Show me your network, and I'll show you your future.

THE NEXT PILLAR in the D.R.E.A.M.™ Job Profile addresses **Relationships**. Having the right people in your corner can mean the difference between staying stuck for years in a role misaligned with your skills and gifts and catapulting to the highest heights of success. The ability to foster genuine, high-quality connections is a hallmark of thriving in the corporate world.

It's disheartening to hear from my clients how difficult it can be to build these types of meaningful relationships at work. A survey conducted by Harvard Business Review found that, even at companies that profess equity and inclusivity, women of color still don't feel supported. (Harvard Business Review, 2019). Challenges we face include being judged through damaging stereotypes and false assumptions about who we are and our backgrounds. Some women have experienced being asked (both directly and indirectly) to conform to the norms related to dress, speech, and temperament of their work environments, so they can "blend in." It can be hard to build professional relationships where we can genuinely express ourselves and be emotionally vulnerable.

Even though building work relationships may be an area especially challenging for you, I want to invite you to think strategically about how the relationships with your colleagues are helping (or hindering) your growth. I've learned when it comes to maximizing your impact, it's not enough for you to know how amazing you are and how much value you bring to the table. Other people have to know, feel, and share these sentiments about you as well. Otherwise, you'll continue to be the best-kept secret at your company.

You can be the best operations manager, the best account executive, the best HR professional, the best lawyer, or the best accountant. If your managers, colleagues, and other key decision-makers at your company aren't aware of how much value you bring to the table and don't feel invested in your growth and success, then it doesn't matter. To tap into opportunities that will help you propel your career to the next level, building strategic relationships is key.

Before we dive into how to do that, let's walk through the various types of work relationships to focus on.

Relationships with Managers

The benefits of a positive relationship with your manager include feeling happier and more content at work, increased motivation, a seat at the decision-making table, and access to growth opportunities, raises, and promotions. Having a difficult relationship with your manager, on the other hand, can break your career.

One of my clients, a senior vice president based in Utah, was hired to lead the diversity & inclusion strategy at a large company. Unfortunately, she had a manager who was determined to undermine her at every turn. My client's manager shot down each idea she presented and excluded her from strategic meetings with senior leadership. When my client was able to launch impactful initiatives at the company, despite being sabotaged, her manager stole the credit! No matter how my client tried to navigate the relationship, things didn't change. It was clear she had no chance of making the kind of impact she was capable of staying on that team. She ultimately resigned.

Relationships with Peers

The relationship with your peers is just as important as the relationship with your manager. Positive relationships with your coworkers lead to higher job satisfaction, increased innovation, and more creativity. Liking your colleagues is also linked to fostering more collaborative and mutually beneficial work outcomes.

I coached a client who had recently landed a mid-level individual contributor role at a small tech company in New York. She was a subject matter expert and had almost 10 years of experience in her field. She assumed the onboarding process for her new role would be seamless since she could do the work with her eyes closed. Unfortunately, this wasn't the case. She didn't anticipate having a rough time connecting with her new peers. She experienced her colleagues as unwelcoming and didn't have anything in common with them. She felt like an outsider, which caused her to isolate herself from the team. This resulted in a lack of support and trust from her peers, as well as decreased reliability.

First, we worked on reframing how she viewed the team dynamics. Instead of taking their lack of welcome activities or onboarding as a personal attack against her, she realized that since the team didn't hire often, they weren't prepared to onboard her onto the team. Although this realization didn't excuse their behavior, it gave her the context she needed to try to salvage the relationships. She worked to establish new norms and communication channels with her coworkers which allowed her to have regular touchpoints where she could build rapport and get to know her team better. It took some time, but eventually she cultivated strong relationships with her manager and another person on the team, and cordial relationships with everyone else.

Other Relationships

In addition to relationships with your manager and coworkers, it's helpful to be intentional about building relationships with mentors, sponsors, workplace partners, professional influencers, and even individuals outside of your company. All of these individuals can be integral to your success journey. Fostering these types of relationships ensures you have the support, air cover, and guidance you need to succeed at work.

To build these relationships, however, it's best to have a base-level understanding of how to network. You may not be a big fan of networking, but it's a key part of thriving in the corporate world, especially for women of color. A lot of my clients initially think networking is tedious or a waste of time. They feel it's inauthentic and that in order to be good at it, you have to change the way you dress, the way you speak, or laugh at jokes you don't find funny. It's important to understand that it's not just what you know that will help you thrive in your career, but it's also about who you know and who knows you.

Let's talk through some of the common misconceptions I've heard about networking.

1. **Networking is arrogant self-promotion.** Networking isn't about selling yourself or trying to impress everyone with all your achievements. This myth claims that you have to put yourself out there and say, "Look at me. Look at what I've done. Pay attention to me. Pick

me." The truth is, when done strategically, networking is just highlighting the relevant achievements you've had in your career, so the right people - those who can influence your trajectory - understand what you've accomplished and how they can support you in getting to your next level.

2. **Networking is a tedious, robotic numbers game.** Networking isn't about racking up all the connections and business cards that you can. You'll want to focus on quality over quantity. Your objective is to build mutually beneficial relationships that will serve you over the trajectory of your career.

3. **Networking means being fake.** I often hear that to be good at networking, you have to be phony. You have to say the things you think people want to hear for them to connect with you. What I've found is the more transparent and genuine you are, the better quality of relationships you're able to build.

Here's the networking approach I've used myself and with my clients to tap into new jobs, speaking engagements, board assignments, and many other game-changing opportunities.

1. **Identify your networking goal.** What kinds of relationships will help you achieve your goals over the next

12 months? Get clear on who you need to know and who needs to know you.

2. **Organize your connections.** Make a list of the people, both inside and outside your company, with whom you want to build relationships. Connections can be made in a variety of ways depending on the individual you're connecting with, whether you have any connections in common, and other variables. Identify the goal you have in mind for the connection. Determine the way you'll make contact with the individuals on your list.

3. **Reach out strategically and consistently.** Use a spreadsheet to keep track of your connections' contact information, date of last touchpoint, and any notes you think are important to remember. Make sure you're checking in at a regular cadence appropriate for the kind of connection you're trying to build. Some connections can stay strong with a semi-annual check-in. For other connections, it makes more sense to check in monthly.

The specifics of your interactions with each individual will vary, but it should all be rooted in cultivating a mutually beneficial relationship in which you're both giving and receiving value and support.

If you're thinking that all you need to do is just show up to work, put your head down, get your work done, and you'll be fine, I hope you're starting to understand how crucial it is for you to incorporate relationship building into your routine. It's no coincidence that the people who are getting the opportunities, getting promoted, getting paid, and getting noticed, are people who are prioritizing building relationships. This is a major key to designing your dream career.

Career Reflection

How would you describe your relationship with your manager, peers, and other key individuals in your career?

How have your work relationships positively or negatively impacted the current state of your career?

How will strategically cultivating professional relationships in the next 12 months help you increase your impact at work?

How have your thoughts about networking impacted your approach to relationship building in your career?

CHAPTER 6

Where You Spend Your Time

The moment you realize you deserve
every good thing you desire is the moment
your environment will begin to shift.

MOST OF MY clients spend more time with their coworkers than they do with the people they live with. That's why the third pillar of the D.R.E.A.M.™ Job Profile, **Environment**, is so important.

When I start working with new clients, we assess how they feel about their work environment, which consists of both the physical environment as well as the intangible, cultural environment.

Physical Environment

Have you thought about what the ideal physical space must include for you to do your best work? If you haven't, don't worry. Most of my clients hadn't given it much thought either before we started working together.

A couple of years ago, I asked the members of my online community to describe their ideal physical work environment. The responses were as varied as the women who submitted them. Their requests included things like lots of healthy food options, bright colorful artwork and decor, and no cubicles.

Though I received diverse responses, there were overarching themes. The most common environmental needs to be met were:

1. A clean and bright environment that inspires productivity

2. Easy access to tools and spaces that foster collaboration with coworkers

3. Ample spaces for quiet, independent work and thinking

Take some time to think about your ideal physical environment. Ask yourself, *What type of environment is going to give me the most energy? What environment is going to make me feel like I can command the room and control the day? What environment will make me feel that I can show up as my best self fully and in the best possible way?*

Cultural Environment

The 12 months I endured that toxic team was in one of the most beautiful office buildings I've ever worked in. It had floor-to-ceiling windows, custom, high-end artwork, an expansive courtyard, and state-of-the-art computer equipment. A toxic work culture can destroy even the most beautiful physical environment.

As a former HR leader and current workplace inclusion consultant, I've had countless conversations about company culture. What I've realized is that most people have no clue how to define it. They see it as this intangible, abstract thing and, though they can't put their finger on it, they know culture impacts how employees feel about the company they work for.

Does culture mean dress code? Is it free food or unlimited vacation days?

I've coined the **3Ps of Work Culture** as a way to describe the core elements:

1. **Perspectives** - the points of view that make up company thinking

2. **Processes** - the systems and structures that drive action within a company

3. **Practices** - the spoken and unspoken behavioral norms in the workplace

To thrive in your career, it's best to find a company whose perspectives, processes, and practices allow you to be seen, heard, valued, and secure. Research tells us that women of color, particularly Black women and Latinas, do not feel these things at work. This is across various companies, levels, locations, and industries (*Women in the Workplace 2020*, 2020). However, this doesn't mean it's impossible. If you're crystal clear about what kind of culture you need to do your best work, you're less likely to walk blindly into a toxic work environment (and less likely to stay should your team suddenly turn into one).

Before joining a new team or company, schedule informational interviews with individuals already there to get a sense of the perspectives, processes, and practices that make up the culture. What are the cultural norms at both the team and organizational levels? What kinds of behaviors get rewarded and punished? Create a list of questions related to inclusion and belonging that you can ask your future boss and colleagues. I often wonder what response I would've gotten had I asked my toxic boss strategic questions during my interview. *What will the onboarding process look like given I don't have HR-specific experience? How do you like to give and receive feedback? Would you describe the team as having a healthy culture of feedback? Why or why not?*

Too many times, we don't think about how important the specifics of physical and cultural environments are until we're in a situation that we do not like. We end up in a physical space that drains our energy and doesn't inspire creativity, a cultural space that alienates and excludes us, or a miserable combination of the two. When designing your dream career, be clear on your needs and actively seek out spaces that align with those requirements.

Career Reflection

Describe your ideal physical work environment?

What can you change about your current physical environment to bridge any gaps between your current and ideal state?

Describe your ideal cultural work environment? How does your current company measure up to your ideal culture?

Do you think you can find a work environment where you're seen, heard, valued, and made to feel secure? Why or why not?

CHAPTER 7

Toot Your Own Horn

*It's not enough for you to know how
much value you bring to the table; other
people must know it as well.*

THE FOURTH PILLAR in the D.R.E.A.M.™ Job Profile is **Acknowledgment.** As human beings, we have an innate need to be acknowledged. We all want to be seen and celebrated. Based on the stories I've heard from my clients, there are many work environments that haven't yet figured out how to meet this need for women of color.

We already experience the workplace less favorably than our white counterparts (*Women in the Workplace 2020*, 2020), the added slight of not being recognized for a job well done can feel like an employer is pouring salt on the various wounds we're already nursing.

I hear stories often about women who consistently work their proverbial fingers to the bone producing the kind of results that make their managers, teams, departments, and companies look good, only to feel unappreciated, undervalued, and taken advantage of. Part of the reason for this is that many of the environments my clients work in are racist, inequitable, and toxic. Fortunately, in spite of less-than-ideal work cultures, there's often an opportunity to teach the people you work with how to celebrate you by tooting your own horn first. It's less likely you'll be celebrated for the great work you do if no one knows you're doing it.

How to Get the Acknowledgement You Deserve

The first step to getting recognition is to get clear. Take the time to understand what kind of acknowledgement you need to feel like your contributions are appreciated. Ask yourself: *In what ways do I want to be recognized for the great work I do? Am I motivated by awards and certificates? Would I prefer my manager send a quick email expressing thanks or making an announcement in front of the team? Do I want a special bonus? Do I prefer being rewarded with stretch assignments and additional responsibility?*

Once you're clear about the kind of acknowledgement you need, your next step is to start giving it to yourself first. How can you expect others to acknowledge how great you are if you're unwilling to acknowledge it yourself? When was the last time you patted yourself on the back?

An assignment I love to give my clients is to create their own "brag folder." A brag folder is a way to keep track of all your career "wins." You can use a physical journal, a virtual folder, or any other preferred tool. The goal is to document the win, the date, and the impact your win has had on your team, department, company, and/or industry. Examples of wins include successfully presenting your findings for a project you're working on, coming up with a solution for a problem your company is facing, or getting promoted. You also want to include any thank you notes or kudos you receive from colleagues.

Set recurring dates to read through your folder, so your accomplishments are always top of mind. It's important for you to celebrate your wins, no matter how small. Take yourself on a lunch date. Buy a bottle of champagne. Do whatever you need to in order to mark the occasion.

Once you've defined acknowledgment on your terms and started the habit of celebrating yourself, you're ready to prime your boss and colleagues so they are aware of your value and are in a position to acknowledge your contributions.

This part of the process consists of two action items:

1. Regularly share your top accomplishments with key stakeholders (i.e., managers, leadership team, human resources, etc.). They should know what work you're

doing, what key milestones you've crossed, and what the impact of the work you're doing entails.

Again, if you're not tooting your own horn, you can't get mad if others don't do it for you.

Here's an example of how you can structure your update:

a. The main 1-2 projects you're working on *(This quarter I'm focused on partnering with the sales team to create a training plan for the new Artificial Intelligence products that have launched.)*

b. The key milestones you've crossed *(I met with the project team yesterday and provided feedback based on the survey the User Experience team conducted. I'm confident we'll meet next month's deadline as planned.)*

c. The impact the work is making *(I was speaking to the head of sales about the priority client they've just acquired who's eagerly awaiting our sales team's ability to onboard the new products. I'm thrilled to be leading the efforts of getting the sales team fully trained on the new product suite.)*

2. Have a candid conversation with your manager about what you need to feel like your work is valued. Once

you and your manager agree about how your contributions will be recognized, it's up to you to hold him or her accountable by speaking up when you're not being recognized. Don't be afraid to remind your manager of the agreement you previously made.

Your need for acknowledgment is valid and a key part of designing your dream career. Try to align yourself with teams and companies that prioritize the recognition of all their employees, particularly women of color. You can do this by paying attention to how past and present women of color describe working there, asking specific questions related to employee recognition during interviews, and carefully observing for yourself how women of color are celebrated and acknowledged.

Career Reflection

What have you been taught about seeking recognition for a job well done in the past?

How comfortable are you talking about your wins and accomplishments? Why do you think that is the case?

When was the last time you felt truly recognized, seen, and acknowledged for the work you do? What happened to make you to feel this way?

What's the one thing you're most proud of throughout your career?

CHAPTER 8

Pad Your Bank Account

Your paycheck reflects more than just the number your company has agreed to pay you. On a deeper level, it reflects what you feel about how much you deserve to earn.

THE FINAL STEP in designing your D.R.E.A.M.™ Job Profile is creating a strategic plan for your **Money**. Based on your education, credentials, experience, and "secret sauce" (we'll define later), how can you maximize your long-term earning potential? What's the highest possible income you can expect to receive based on your position and industry. What's your plan to get there? The answers to these questions inform your compensation strategy.

We've spent three chapters talking about how important the right mindset is when it comes to career success. Your relationship to money and your beliefs about what you can earn have a direct impact on your financial outcomes.

Fresh out of college, we tend to just be excited to have a job. We don't think too much about how our salary will impact our career long-term. Your initial salary creates the baseline for everything else you'll be paid in your lifetime. I wish I'd known this earlier in my career. It took me 6 years before I ever broached the topic of money with a manager. When I did, my negotiation "strategy" was sloppy. I didn't prepare for the conversation ahead of time and didn't have a concrete outcome in mind. I'd done no research and wasn't equipped to have a meaningful conversation about the rationale for me wanting a raise.

It wasn't until I took the time to research the market rate for my role, get clear on how to define the value I was bringing to the team, and actively worked to shift my thoughts on how much I was worthy of earning, that things started to take off. I've been able to negotiate multiple 5-figure raises for myself including one increase of $45,000. I've helped my clients negotiate huge raises, too. As I'm writing this, the current record is a $90,000 increase for a client in HR policy.

It's important to know that there's more to compensation than just your salary. When thinking about your ideal pay, it's best to think of it in terms of total compensation, both direct and indirect.

Direct compensation is monetary payment in exchange for your contributions. Indirect compensation are the various types of non-monetary pay that companies give to employees (i.e., healthcare benefits, life insurance, childcare, free food, etc.). For the purpose of this exercise, let's focus on direct compensation. Here's what it can entail:

1. **Salary** - fixed compensation paid at a regular cadence

2. **Commission** - variable compensation paid as a percentage of sales or revenue

3. **Bonus** - variable compensation that can be paid as a flat rate or percentage of salary

4. **Equity** - non-cash compensation in the form of investment vehicles which may include options, restricted stock, and performance shares

I often hear people say it's not possible to live a lavish lifestyle and build wealth working a 9-5 job. Meanwhile, one of my friends, a diversity & inclusion executive living in Atlanta, Georgia is quietly sitting on millions of dollars in equity from the various companies she's worked for. She can cash in on her stock at any time and do with it as she pleases. This is in addition to her multiple six-figure salary, annual bonus, board stipend, and paid speaking engagements.

Another woman, a Tech recruiter living in New York City, was able to use the proceeds of her stock options as a down payment for her first home. I was able to become debt free, travel to many countries (sometimes first class if I'm feeling spicy) and provide an extremely comfortable lifestyle for my family in two of the most expensive cities in the country with my corporate job. There are countless stories like these, and there is no reason that you can't do the same thing.

The first step to creating your compensation strategy is to assess where you are. According to a 2019 survey by Robert Half, 46% of employees feel they're under-compensated. Based on my experience with women of color, I'd argue the percentage is possibly higher if we cut the data by race and gender.

There's a difference between generally feeling like you're not making enough to save, invest, or travel and having the intel to back up these thoughts. Having concrete data to stand on is an important step in crafting your compensation strategy.

Start by asking yourself these three questions:

1. **Has my level of responsibility increased, but my compensation has stayed the same?** In general, when your responsibilities increase, your compensation should too. If there's been a significant change in what's expected of you, a conversation on how the change affects your compensation is warranted.

2. **Have I received a raise within the past 12 months?** In an ideal world, it would be realistic to expect to receive a raise every year. Not only to keep up with the rate of

inflation, but also to represent the value you've contributed to your team over the previous 12 months.

3. **Do I know [for a fact] people in similar roles to me are being compensated at a higher level?** While your employer may prefer otherwise, it's not illegal for you to discuss pay with your co-workers. Check in with your community and keep your research up to date. Include data points from individuals of diverse racial backgrounds. On average, women of color get paid less than their white counterparts (*Quick Facts About the Gender Wage Gap*, 2020), so it's helpful to not only know what other women of color are making, but what your white colleagues are making as well.

Once you've reflected on your answers, it's time to create your plan to close the gap between your current compensation and the highest possible income you can expect to receive in the future.

1. Assess the current state of your total compensation as well as your trajectory for the past 5 - 10 years. Remember, you're not only looking at your salary, but you're also looking at the other types of direct compensation as well.

2. Do your research so you're clear on where you fall in the market. Diversify your data collection by relying on various inputs. Try career sites like Glassdoor and

LinkedIn. Speak with recruiters at other companies, human resources representatives at your company, and individuals from various gender and racial groups who have similar experience and are in similar roles.

3. Identify your non-negotiables and the minimum expectations you have for total compensation based on your background, education, credentials, and industry.

4. Create a timeline, complete with key milestones along the way, that outlines the specific steps you will take to bridge the gap between your current and target compensation.

5. Determine what your next steps will be if your employer is unable to meet your compensation needs.

As you solidify your compensation plan, it may become clear you're going to have to negotiate for higher pay, either by speaking with your manager about an adjustment and/or promotion or by securing a higher paying role at another company.

Below is a high-level overview of how to approach negotiating your compensation during a job search.

1. **Know your numbers.** As I've previously mentioned, it's important to enter a negotiation with a clear picture of what your market value is and what additional value should be added based on your specific qualifications.

Determine your target compensation before launching your job search.

2. **Avoid the topic for as long as possible.** It seems counterintuitive, but it's best to discuss compensation *after* you've received a job offer. You give yourself more leverage to negotiate once you know you're the "chosen one".

Many states and cities including Massachusetts, California, New York City, New Orleans, Pittsburgh, and Philadelphia have passed laws that ban state agencies and certain employers from asking about your current or previous salary (Janove, 2019). The ban helps narrow the gender pay gap. Do your research so you can know the latest updates surrounding equal pay legislation in your area.

Potential employers are allowed to ask what your salary expectations are going forward. Try to avoid answering for as long as you can. If you're asked the question on a job application, you can write, "I look forward to discussing compensation once I've learned more about the position." You also can say, "My previous salary was below market value, and I look forward to learning more about the role and discussing compensation based on my skill set, experience, and market value." If the application requires you to input a number, you can consider writing "$1". That way you satisfy the system requirement of providing a numerical input but avoid putting your actual salary requirements.

If you're being asked your expectations via phone or video call, you can try one of the below responses:

- "Salary isn't the number one motivating factor for me right now. I'm excited about the challenges and opportunities this company and position offer, and I'm sure when the time is right, and if this is a perfect fit for both of us, we'll decide on a compensation package we're all happy with. Could you tell me more about [a question related to the position]?"
- "Right now, I'm more focused on finding the perfect fit for what I'm seeking next in my career. I'm looking for a company that aligns with my values, and where I can bring results to the team. Which is what has attracted me to [company name]. Could you tell me more about [a question related to the position]?"
- "My previous salary was below market value. I would like my next salary to match my skill set, experience, and qualifications. I would love to learn more about the budget set for this position.

3. **Negotiate from a place of power.** A key step in the negotiation process is framing your contributions in a

way that lets the employer know that you understand the value you bring to the table, as well as the market rate for your role.

Here are a few phrases you can use when negotiating your compensation.

- "In my previous position, I was able to [insert your best accomplishments]. I am confident that I will be able to do the same and more in this position. That said, for me to make a move, I'd need to receive a [insert compensation here]."
- "After doing my research, I discovered that the average pay for someone at my level with my qualifications is [insert compensation here]."
- "Based on my experience and research of positions with a similar level of responsibility and scope, I'm seeking a salary range of [insert target range]."

Getting in the driver's seat of your compensation is deeper than just being able to pad your bank account for the sake of it. Increasing your compensation also means you can save and invest more, show your loved ones what knowing your worth looks like, leave a nest egg for your children, and do the fun things you've always wanted to do.

Shifting from survivor mode into thriver status becomes possible when you're crystal clear on what you need to have a dream career. The D.R.E.A.M.™ Job Profile provides the tools and language necessary to define what that looks like for you. Taking the time to craft your profile means you can start making D.R.E.A.M.™ decisions. These are the kind of decisions made from a space of triumph instead of trauma. They are rooted in your personal definition of success. D.R.E.A.M.™ decisions move you further away from simply going through the motions in your career and force you to stop merely existing at work and start living.

Career Reflection

How have your beliefs about what you can earn in your career impacted your current compensation?

What emotions come up for you when talking about your salary? Why do you think that is?

When's the last time you brought up compensation to your employer? What was the outcome?

How much would you like to earn in the next 12 months? Why is this number important to you?

PART 3

Thrive Everyday

CHAPTER 9

Set Smarter Goals

*Don't expect to reap successful
outcomes if you're not willing to
sow successful actions.*

WE'VE SPENT THE previous five chapters designing the plan for your dream career. Now that you know what you want, it's time to set goals to get there.

The concept of setting goals isn't a new one, but what I've noticed with the women I speak with is that while they know how to set goals, they're often unable to stay on track to accomplish those goals. The main reason for this is the lack of a structured goal setting system. The corporate world can be a cold, hard place for us. It can be difficult and challenging to come in day after day and deal with moving goalposts, empty promises, and things not happening in the way we think they should. If you don't have a process in place that's going to keep you on track, you're not going to move forward. You're going to stay stagnant.

You may have heard the importance of setting "SMART goals." SMART is an acronym meaning goals are to be **Specific, Measurable, Actionable, Realistic**, and **Time-bound**. In my experience, a lot of high-achieving women of color know what SMART goals are, but they still find it incredibly challenging to accomplish them. To fix that, I like to introduce the concept of **SMARTer** goals to my clients.

What are SMARTer Goals?

The "S" in SMARTer goals stands for **Sexy**. Sexy goals make you feel warm and tingly on the inside. If you don't feel inspired by your goals and don't feel motivated to jump out of bed and do the things you need to do in order to accomplish them, it's likely they're not sexy. It doesn't matter if anyone else cares about your goals or is inspired by them. Do they inspire YOU? Do YOU smile when you think about them? A turning point in my career was when I moved away from basic, boring ambitions, and started going after goals I actually could get excited about. I committed to setting objectives that motivated me. When I opened my eyes in the morning and contemplated hitting the snooze button on my phone, I would say to myself, "Oh no, I've got work to do," and jump out the bed ready to do the work necessary to complete my goal.

The "M" stands for **Meaningful**. In addition to being sexy, your goals should mean something to you. They should have a clear "why" that's aligned with your core values and your measures of success. If you set goals like: "I want to get promoted", or "I want to connect with that person", and they aren't aligned to anything deeper, you're not going to stay motivated. Additionally, you won't feel anything when you eventually reach your goals because they didn't mean much to you in the first place.

The "A" stands for **Aspirational**. Ideally, you want your goals to take you out of your comfort zone. It's great if they feel like a bit of a stretch and make you think, *This is exciting. It's also kind of scary.* If the goals you set are easy for you to accomplish or attain, they likely aren't aspirational. Aspirational goals are what's going to get you to muster up the strength and courage to face the challenges of the corporate world.

The "R" stands for **Real**. Be sure your goal is what *you* want and not what someone else wants you to accomplish. I don't care which friend or family member wants you to be a doctor, get a certain degree, work in a particular industry, or go and quit your job to pursue the next big thing. Once you identify what success looks like on your terms, that is the space from which you should create your goals.

The "T" is for **Time-sensitive**. Goals that make you feel a sense of urgency to get them done because you just can't wait to accomplish them are what you're aiming for. Think about it, if you're okay with taking two years to accomplish something that really could have been accomplished in six months or 12 months, is this an exciting, sexy goal? You want to be thinking, *This is something that I want, so I'm going to do what I need to do to accelerate my path to the finish line.*

Crafting Your SMARTer Goals

Now that you understand what SMARTer goals are, it's time for you to create some of your own. Go back to your responses to previous career reflection questions and consolidate the list of goals you've outlined for the next phase of your career.

Determine which 2 -3 goals will be your focus and write them down. Make sure each goal is not only SMART, but also SMARTer.

Here are some examples of SMARTer goals:

- I am a recognized thought leader and expert on growth marketing strategies. I will complete 2 paid speaking engagements and sign 1 consulting client by September 15.
- I have landed a new position that leverages my strengths in marketing and communications with an organization that aligns with my values, goals and work style within the next 6 months. This new position will come with a raise of at least $35,000.

- I will be promoted to VP in the next promotion cycle (12 months from now). My new title will be accompanied with a relocation to New York City, a 15% salary increase, as well as managerial responsibilities.

Making Time for Your Goals

It's not enough just to set goals and forget them. You have to go about doing the work to accomplish them. One thing that I hear a lot from my clients is, *"I don't have the time to go after my goals. There's so much that is expected of me both inside and outside of work. Though I genuinely want to thrive in my career, show up as an expert and a thought leader, and accomplish all the goals I've set, I'm having trouble finding the time to make it happen."*

The demands many of us have on our time are overwhelming. To accomplish your SMARTer goals and set yourself up to thrive in your dream career though, you'll have to create the time and space, both physically and mentally, to make your goals happen. Start by tracking your schedule for 7 days and take note of how you're spending your time. Are there tasks that you can deprioritize while you work on your goals? Are there activities you can eliminate altogether? Is it possible to sacrifice a few hours of sleep or outsource some of your obligations while you focus on your goals? When my clients tell me they want to pursue their career goals but they simply "don't have time," my response is and will always be, "Then, you must create the time."

It boils down to this question: "Are your goals a priority to you right now or not?"

If the answer is "no," that's okay. Understand it's going to take a lot longer to accomplish the goals that you've set and there's the possibility you may never achieve them. That's not a judgment, it's just what "no" means.

If the answer is "yes," then you must decide that you'll do what it takes to create the time and space you need. You've taken the time to identify what you want and define what success looks like to you. You've mapped out your goals. Now, it's time to do the work.

Career Reflection

What goal-setting process(es) have you used in the past to help you achieve your goals? What was the outcome?

How can crafting goals that are both SMART and SMARTer help you stay on track to build a fulfilling career?

What will you do differently to ensure that you're able to create the time and space needed to accomplish your career goals?

How will you hold yourself accountable on your journey to accomplishing your career goals?

CHAPTER 10

Find Your Secret Sauce

*You have been intentionally and
specifically created to do great work.*

A S YOU CONTINUE on this journey of designing the kind of career in which you can make more
money, have more impact, and thrive, it's important
to ensure you're showing up in a way that clearly communicates
to others you're aware you belong in the rooms in which you
find yourself. In order to do that, you'll need to get crystal clear
about what your **VIP** is – which is your **Value**, your **Impact**,
and your **Power**. Let's walk through what your **VIP** represents.

Defining Your Value

Your value is the specific contributions you make to the overall growth of your team, department, and/or company. It represents the unique skills, perspectives, and experiences that you bring to the table and the activities you manage that make the spaces you're a part of better.

A great way to zone in on your specific value is to ask yourself, *How do I contribute to the company's bottom line?* In addition to bringing in revenue, contributing to the bottom line also can mean saving money, saving time, building culture, and positively impacting the company's reputation. Contributing to the bottom line also can mean doing work for a team or department that is responsible for achieving a company goal. Ask yourself, *Am I serving customers? Am I helping my company build better relationships?* It is not just about money. Even if you don't have a dollar amount specifically tied to the work you do, there's still value that you're bringing to the table.

Most of my clients aren't revenue producers. Their roles span administrative functions like operations, legal, HR, marketing, or communications, and they're still able to articulate clearly and confidently how the work they do helps produce results that positively impact the company's bottom line.

Assessing Your Impact

Your impact speaks to how you *quantify* your value, and it represents the number of people, products, regions, etc. that your work influences. Your impact not only can be measured numerically, but also can be global or domestic. It can be internal or external. There's no "right" or "wrong" way to quantify your value. Just because the impact you have is on hundreds of people, and someone else's work impacts millions of people doesn't make one better than the other.

Sometimes, when I'm working with a client to help position her impact, I'll hear something like, *"Well, I only have three direct reports. My team is too small."* She may say, *"I only supported 20 customers. That's so little, so I'm not sure it's worth including."* Here's the thing: All your experience matters, and you get to decide how you want to package your greatness.

Standing in Your Power

Your power is how you intentionally and deliberately choose to *own* your value and impact. Once you've identified the value you bring and the impact that your work has, are you making a deliberate effort to walk in it every day? How do you speak (or not speak) about your contributions and achievements? Are you standing up to those who seek to belittle or undermine your contributions?

I've seen time and time again where the women I encounter are less likely to powerfully share their value and impact with the key stakeholders in their careers (i.e., managers, senior leaders, and influencers). They're more likely to keep to themselves the fact that they're single-handedly running a territory or producing work that saves the company thousands, millions, or even billions of dollars. Your ability to stand in your power is how you signal to your colleagues that you're aware of how your contributions add value.

Find Your Secret Sauce

While your VIP is what your contributions are, your secret sauce is how you go about making your contributions happen.

Your secret sauce can be uncovered by mining through all the experiences you've had in the past, the value and impact that you bring to the table, and your personality so you can flesh out your unique expertise.

I've worked with enough women to know it can be challenging to consolidate decades of experience in a way that accurately and powerfully reflects your unique expertise. It's easy to forget what you've accomplished and it's easy to dismiss the skills we don't use every single day.

I've designed the following exercise to help jog your memory.

1. **Make a list of all your past roles** (even the ones that no longer seem relevant). Pull out your resume and/or

LinkedIn profile and start by answering the following questions. *What are the projects or special assignments in which I have participated or led? What are the names of the companies for whom I've worked? In what industries was the focus of my work?* These are just questions to get the juices flowing. Write down anything that helps paint the picture of the kind of work you've done throughout your career.

2. **Zone in on your skills.** Write down your answers to the following questions: *In what area(s) am I particularly proficient? In what area(s) do people come to me for help? Am I known as the go-to resource for help in a specific area? What skills do I see repeatedly through my work history?*

3. **Tap into your interests.** You may begin to see themes emerging about the work you do and your skills. Take it a step further by asking yourself: *What are my passions? What are my areas of interest? What are my values? What do I like to learn? What do I like to read? What podcasts do I enjoy? What do I watch? Do I hold a core value that I would prefer to share with the people with whom I work?*

4. **Incorporate your personality.** I don't know about you, but I'm tired of the narrative that says I have to be fake or put on a certain persona to climb the corporate ladder. In this final part of the process, ask yourself:

Which core characteristics of my personality do I treasure most? What quirks do I have that make me more effective in my career? What words do those who know me best use to describe me?

Once you've gone through and made notes for each part of the process, it's time to distill it all down into one or two sentences that capture the essence of who you are and what you bring to the table professionally.

The formula I like to use to help my clients articulate their secret sauce is I'm a [insert forward-looking title that captures where you want to go next in your career] who leverages [insert unexpected, but relevant skill set] to [insert how you impact the bottom line]. You get bonus points if you're able to incorporate a personality trait.

Here are a few examples of secret sauce statements:

- I'm an operations manager who leverages my coaching background to help high-growth teams implement time-saving systems.
- I'm a middle school teacher turned account executive who uses humor and above-average persuasion skills to make companies a lot of money.
- I'm a data-driven human resources leader who uses the power of kindness and connection to improve employee morale.

Feel free to tweak the formula any way you see fit. The key is to talk about your value, impact, and unique expertise in a way that not only feels authentic to you but also instills confidence in your ability to perform to others. This is your secret sauce.

Career Reflection

What's the most recent compliment you've received from your manager, your colleagues, or your client? Which of your core skills does this compliment highlight?

What's the most impactful idea you've suggested that improved outcomes for your team?

How can the ability to articulate your secret sauce help position you for bigger and better career opportunities in the future?

What can you do to increase the impact you're making in your current role?

CHAPTER 11

Take Up Space

Give yourself permission to stand in your power
and authority today and every day.

EVERY YEAR, I host an intimate, six-month career success incubator for senior-level women of color who want to leverage their experience and expertise to become a sought-after voice in their field. It's called *The Launchpad*, and the women who graduate from each cohort go on to secure paid speaking engagements, land press and podcast features, publish viral thought leadership content, and land five and six-figure consulting gigs. At the start of each cohort, I always ask participants to tell me what topics they want to make sure we cover during our time together. Of all the topics that they request, the one that comes up most often is executive presence.

"You need to work on your executive presence". This phrase single-handedly has stalled the careers of many women of color and kept them from climbing the corporate ladder. The issue isn't about feedback in and of itself. Feedback is a good thing. The problem is that quite often, telling women of color to "work on your executive presence" is a euphemism for, *You're not assimilating well enough into our culture. I need you to change.* What's worse is that most of the time my clients are given this feedback, it's not accompanied by any concrete action steps they can take to "improve". It's not surprising, then, that even the members of *The Launchpad*, with all their experience, accolades, and credentials, are still unsure of how to tackle this nebulous concept.

Understanding Executive Presence

Executive presence is the ability to inspire confidence in others. It's how your managers, your peers, your subordinates, and your clients perceive your ability to do your job well. You can't touch or hold executive presence. It's abstract. Unlike presentation skills or being able to code, you can't demonstrate your proficiency in executive presence easily. It's one of those things you mostly hear about when things are *not* going well.

Executive presence can be distilled into three distinct parts: communication, appearance, and gravitas. Let's dig into each category to better understand how to leverage executive presence in your career.

Communication

Your ability to communicate clearly, confidently, and concisely will make or break others' perceptions of you. When you communicate, you want to make sure you've thought about how your audience will process what you've shared. Ask yourself, *What is the objective? What's my point? What do I want my audience to take away? What decisions should my audience be able to make after we've concluded our exchange?*

Aim for your communication to be as concise as possible. *How can I get my thoughts across in the most seamless way?* You're not going to rush or leave out relevant talking points. Instead, you want to focus solely on giving your audience the information they need and removing the fluff.

Finally, you must be confident. The easiest way to increase your confidence is to be prepared. Research the topics your manager cares about, so you can engage in conversation the next time you meet. Scan the meeting agenda in advance, so you can chime in strategically during the meeting.

As you work to cultivate your executive presence, improving communication must be a foundational part of your process.

Appearance

Appearance is how you present yourself physically. This can mean anything from how you dress to how you organize your backdrop for virtual meetings.

I want to clarify that when I'm speaking about appearance here, it's not about conforming or assimilating. Instead, appearance, in the context of maximizing your executive presence, is all about doing what you need to in order to feel and look your most confident. There is a world in which you can adhere to your company or industry's norms when it comes to dress, and still can show up fully and authentically. When you feel like you look your best, you're more likely to exude confidence. When you're confident, you're more likely to show up and deliver powerfully.

Focusing on your appearance as a way to build executive presence is about looking in the mirror and knowing that you are completely enough no matter how you look. It's about being comfortable in your skin or body.

Gravitas

Gravitas is a Latin word that means "weight" or "heaviness" and it's about taking up space both literally and figuratively. It's the most intangible of all the components of executive presence. Taking up space looks different for everyone. It can look like owning and stating your opinion even when it differs from everyone else's. Or resisting the urge to apologize to people for things you don't have to be sorry for. Or refusing to shrink yourself to accommodate people who don't show you respect.

Whenever you enter a physical or virtual room, think to yourself, *I am here. I'm here with my big hair and my big earrings. I'm here with my red lipstick and my unique voice. I'm here with my out of the box ideas and my big confidence. I am taking up space. I'm not moving to the side.*

Benefits of a Powerful Presence

Mastering your executive presence is a key part of career success. As an HR executive, I participated in countless conversations with managers about employee performance. Sometimes the only difference between the individuals who were promoted, supported, and amplified and those who weren't boiled down to intangibles like communication, appearance, and gravitas.

A major key to success is your ability to influence what people say about you when you're not in the room. You want the people with whom you work to become ambassadors for you, so they're able to talk about the confidence you instill in them as a leader, a peer, and a valuable contributor to the team.

Career Reflection

How would you describe your executive presence currently? What would you change and why?

How would you describe the executive presence of the individuals at your company or in your industry who are excelling? What common themes do you notice?

What can you do to begin taking up more literal and figurative space at work?

How can you bring more authenticity to the way you show up in the workplace?

CHAPTER 12

The Elephant in the Room

The inability for someone else to
recognize your value doesn't change the fact
that you are, indeed, valuable.

NO CONVERSATION ABOUT women of color in the workplace would be complete without addressing the giant elephant in the room - racism. Racism and racial insensitivity at work are real and negatively impact women of color every single day. Whether it's people questioning your ability to do your work well solely based on your race, receiving the uncomfortable looks and comments when you show up to work wearing, speaking, or being true to your cultural heritage, or even the well-intentioned reassurance from your colleague that "doesn't see race" or that you're lucky we've "overcome" the barriers people of color *used to* face. It's tougher out here for us.

While this book has provided you with the strategies my clients and I have used to circumvent many of the barriers women of color face at work, it's also important to talk about the very real, very discouraging microaggressions.

A microaggression is a comment, action, or environment that negatively targets a historically underrepresented person or group of people. While a great deal of microaggressive behavior is unintentional, they can also be done on purpose. Microaggressions are a form of discrimination, and they're one of the major ways racism and racial insensitivity manifest themselves at work.

Examples of Microaggressions Women of Color Face

- **Having your expertise, competence, or seniority constantly questioned.** I remember going to a leadership conference for HR leaders years ago, and when I arrived at the registration desk before I could even open my mouth, I was told that I should be using the entrance for vendors.

- **Being told to dress, speak, or present yourself in a particular way.** This isn't a slight against being professional, but there's a difference between letting everyone know the dress code and saying to a woman of color, "Are you planning to wear your hair like that to the client meeting? You look more polished when it's straightened and pulled back."

- **Being accused of being angry or emotional.** This is difficult, especially when expressing concern over a racist or racially insensitive comment or action. Many women have told me they're consistently accused of being angry or aggressive simply for voicing their disapproval about something that's happened at work.

These experiences can often lead to self-questioning, guilt, and doubt. Let's walk through some of the common questions you may have asked yourself about microaggressive behavior at work.

1. **Am I being too sensitive?** It's easy to second guess yourself if you're the target of a microaggression, and you may wonder if you're overreacting or overthinking things.

2. **Should I just leave?** Being the recipient of microaggressive comments and actions can create real feelings of misunderstanding, isolation, and hopelessness at work. It may feel like the only way to escape the discomfort is to quit.

3. **Should I speak up?** Whether it's in the moment or after the fact, a lot of us struggle with this question. Depending

on the situation, it can feel risky to self-advocate, and you may be unsure of how to proceed.

4. **Did I do something wrong?** Being on the receiving end of a microaggression can cause you to be overly critical of yourself and your actions. Was I being too loud or too bossy? Was the person who made this remark to me right in some way?

5. **What's my responsibility to others?** You may feel that it's your responsibility to speak up for others and provide education about microaggressions. You also may feel that not doing so is a moral failure on your part.

These questions are normal. Remember that someone else's racist or racially insensitive behavior is 100% about them and not about you.

Facing Racial Microaggressions Head On

One of the fascinating parts of my work as a human resources leader and workplace inclusion consultant is observing how individuals respond when confronted about their microaggressive behavior. It can feel uncomfortable to realize you've offended someone. Many people respond defensively and shift the blame off themselves and onto the person raising the concern.

Psychologist Jennifer Freyd, Ph.D. calls this behavior "DARVO."

1. The offender **Denies** the microaggression ever took place. *(I can't believe you think what I said was offensive. I am not racist. That's not what I meant.)*

2. The offender **Attacks** the victim for attempting to hold them accountable. *(You make everything about race. The fact that you're cornering me and forcing me to have this conversation is making me feel extremely uncomfortable.)*

3. thus, **Reversing Victim** and **Offender.**

Whether you experience microaggressions regularly or as an isolated incident, here are some self-care strategies you can consider using.

1. **Locate Community.** It can be helpful to seek out a community at work either within your organization or within outside networks designed specifically for women of color.

2. **Affirm Yourself.** Microaggressions are based on stereo-types, not reality. Find opportunities to remind yourself of your value. For example, when I'm the recipient of microaggressions that seek to invalidate my experience or question my knowledge, I re-read old performance

reviews, talk to friends and family members who are naturally affirming, and do other things to counter the negative messages I've received.

3. **Validate Your Emotions.** You're not being overly sensitive or wrong for feeling the way you do. Whether you need 30 seconds or 30 hours, you're entitled to think, reflect, and process what has happened. Deliberately and intentionally detach yourself from internalizing any blame or shame from the outcome.

There are many ways to respond to a microaggression. You can choose to ignore it, confront the offender directly, and/ or escalate the situation to someone else. However you choose to address it is valid. Everyone is different, so think about the combination of tactics for responding to microaggressions that feel best for you.

You are not obligated to educate someone who has harmed you. However, if you feel safe enough to confront the person. I want you to have the tools you need to handle the situation appropriately.

A great way to provide feedback is the SBI feedback model from the Center for Creative Leadership, 2019. SBI stands for **Situation**, **Behavior**, and **Impact**. This is a structure for giving feedback that helps you organize your thoughts and represent them in a way that is both factual and expressive of your experiences.

The process goes like this. First, provide context for the situation. Next, describe the behavior or action taken. Finally, discuss the impact of the behavior on you, your colleagues, or the company.

Here's an example: *While we were debriefing about a Black candidate who is eager to join our team, you mentioned your concern that she seemed "too aggressive". The biggest worry you raised was that she might not be a good fit for the role since we are a client facing team. While I understand wanting to find the right teammate to fit what we need, this concern surprised me given everything we heard about her experience and accomplishments in the interview process. As a Black woman who is also assertive, it made me worry about how you perceive me. I also wondered if we would have the same conversation about a white man with the same career goals. As someone I work with often, I wanted you to know the impact on me of what likely felt like a small remark.*

While you can't control how the other person will react, taking this approach helps decrease the likelihood you'll be met with an overly defensive, dismissive, or combative response. If you are, you can rest comfortably in the fact that you did your best to try to promote a respectful and collaborative outcome.

In an ideal situation, you should be able to speak directly with the individual and come to a resolution. However, sometimes, it just isn't an option. Maybe, you've spoken up on various occasions and the microaggressive behavior continues. Or the perpetrator doesn't see what they have said or done as an issue and therefore, they have no intention of changing the behavior.

Or something egregious has happened, and you'd like to report it. In cases like these, you should feel empowered to use the escalation channels at your disposal to ensure that your voice is heard, and your experience is acknowledged.

Career Reflection

Have you ever experienced or witnessed a racial microaggression at work? How did you respond when it happened?

How comfortable are you confronting microaggressions head-on? Why do you think that is the case?

What self-care strategies can you start implementing immediately to help you cope with the microaggressions you face at work?

How do you think your ability to navigate microaggressions at work will impact the likelihood you'll thrive in the corporate world?

Conclusion

NOW THAT YOU'VE read *Deeper Than Work: How Women of Color Can Make More Money, Have More Impact, and Thrive in the Corporate World*, you have the tools you need to show up fully and authentically at work.

You absolutely can cultivate a career in which you bring the very best of yourself to work and still have all the impact, influence, and, of course, income that you deserve.

In this book, I've outlined the strategies necessary to design a career in which you consistently develop and sharpen your skills, build long-lasting, mutually beneficial relationships, thrive in environments that allow you to make a massive impact, receive the recognition and acknowledgment you deserve, and make the kind of money that's aligned with your contributions.

Here's a summary of what I've shared:

Chapter 1: Get Your Mind Right - How to cultivate the kind of mindset you need to take control and dominate your career.

Chapter 2: Confidence is a Choice - How to override the limits you have about what's possible in your career.

Chapter 3: The Path You're Called to Follow - How to define success on your terms and no longer be held prisoner by other people's expectations.

Chapter 4: Plan to Fill the Gaps - How to create a strategic development plan that will position you for success.

Chapter 5: Maximize Your Impact - How to be intentional about the relationships you're cultivating.

Chapter 6: Where You Spend Your Time - How to identify and go after the kind of physical and cultural environments you need to thrive.

Chapter 7: Toot Your Own Horn - How to own your contributions and ensure you're being recognized for the value you provide.

Chapter 8: Pad Your Bank Account - How to create a compensation strategy so you can maximize your earning potential.

Chapter 9: Set Smarter Goals - How to set strategic goals that help to accelerate your success.

Chapter 10: Find Your Secret Sauce - How to uncover and articulate all the value, impact, and power you bring to the table.

Chapter 11: Take Up Space - How to stand in your power and authority every single day.

Chapter 12: The Elephant in the Room - How to navigate microaggressions in the workplace as a woman of color.

Remember, the strategies you've learned in this book won't work unless you implement them.

Don't let your career transformation journey end when you close this book. Try to commit to using at least one strategy I've shared within the next 24 hours and continue from there.

It's time for you to thrive.

About the Author

Dorianne St Fleur went from spending 12 months stuck in a soul-sucking, toxic work environment, to becoming an HR leader for Fortune 500 companies like AT&T and Google.

As a high-performance career coach, corporate trainer, speaker, and sought after thought leader, Dorianne has taken the many lessons learned from over 15 years in Corporate America and used them to help her clients reinvent themselves and their careers. She teaches ambitious women how to gain deeper career clarity, become more visible in their industries, propel into dream roles, and secure huge pay raises.

Dorianne's mission is to eliminate the pay and leadership gaps for women of color in the corporate world. She has spent thousands of hours helping high achievers from the United States, the Caribbean, Canada, and the United Kingdom climb to the heights of success without sacrificing their dignity, identity, or sanity in the process.

Born and raised in Brooklyn, New York, Dorianne currently lives with her husband and daughter in San Jose, California.

Next Steps

Thanks for taking the time to read *Deeper Than Work: How Women of Color Can Make More Money, Have More Impact, and Thrive in the Corporate World*.

If you would like additional support, below are a few options to get you started.

Tools & Resources. For more tools and resources to help you implement the strategies shared in this book, please visit **www.deeperthanwork.com/resources**. You can also listen to the Deeper Than Work podcast at **www.deeperthanwork.com/podcast**.

Leadership Development Coaching. If you are interested in learning more about one-on-one or group coaching, please visit **www.doriannestfleur.co** for information about upcoming masterclasses, coaching programs, incubators, and much more.

Workplace Inclusion Consulting. If you'd like to learn more about how your organization can build an environment that includes, amplifies, and celebrates women of color, please visit **www.doriannestfleur.co**.

Keynotes, Workshops & Corporate Training. Interested in having Dorianne speak at your next event? Please visit **www.doriannestfleur.co**.

References

Freyd, J. J. (1997). Violations of power, adaptive blindness, and betrayal trauma theory. *Feminism & Psychology, 7,* 22–32.

Harvard Business Review. (2019). *Even at "Inclusive" Companies, Women of Color Don't Feel Supported.* https://hbr.org/2019/08/even-at-inclusive-companies-women-of-color-dont-feel-supported

Janove, J. J. D. (2019, October 29). *More Jurisdictions Are Banning Salary-History Inquiries.* SHRM. https://www.shrm.org/resourcesandtools/legal-and-compliance/state-and-local-updates/pages/more-jurisdictions-are-banning-salary-history-inquiries.aspx

Leadership, C. F. C. (2019). *Feedback That Works: How to Build and Deliver Your Message, Second Edition* (Revised ed.). Center for Creative Leadership.

Quick Facts About the Gender Wage Gap. (2020, March 24). Center for American Progress. https://www.american-progress.org/issues/women/reports/2020/03/24/482141/quick-facts-gender-wage-gap/

Robert Half. (2019). *Money Matters: Survey Finds Workers Are Scrutinizing Salaries; Feelings Split On Pay Satisfaction.* https://www.multivu.com/players/English/8217352-robert-half-2020-salary-guides/

Women in the Workplace 2020. (2020). LeanIn.org and McKinsey. https://www.mckinsey.com/featured-insights/diversity-and-inclusion/women-in-the-workplace